BORN TO DIE IN ORDER TO LIVE

|||||||||||||||||||||||||||||||||||
I0150796

Gary J. Davis

TEACH Services, Inc.
P U B L I S H I N G
www.TEACHServices.com • (800) 367-1844

Copyright © 2024 Gary J. Davis
Copyright © 2024 TEACH Services, Inc.
ISBN-13: 978-1-4796-1733-3 (Paperback)
ISBN-13: 978-1-4796-1735-7 (Mass Market)
ISBN-13: 978-1-4796-1734-0 (ePub)

Published by

TEACH Services, Inc.
P U B L I S H I N G
www.TEACHServices.com • (800) 367-1844

TABLE OF CONTENTS

DEDICATION

I dedicate this short autobiography in memory of Mrs. Helen Brown Davis, my deceased mother. Momma had a way of bringing the best out of me. When I told momma that I was thinking about writing my autobiography, she responded, "Gary, you might as well write the book because you have done everything else!" She meant that I had done everything else for the good Lord. So, I write this booklet with fond memories and with what she told me about my writing this booklet in mind.

PREFACE

I praise and give glory to God for allowing me to write this brief auto-biography. I write with the intent of helping all readers to understand that we all are born in need of another life; we are in need of a life filled with righteousness, joy, peace, and serenity that leads to eternal life, which only Jesus can give us. It's a life that replaces sin, sadness, unrighteousness, and misery, and only Jesus Christ can take these away.

I would have each reader to understand and know that we are not authentically living—I mean really living—until we make the essential choice to accept Jesus as our personal Savior from sin. Not only can Jesus give us life but life everlasting as well!

My hope and prayer is that Jesus will bless you as only He can as you continue to read how I was born to die, in order to live, and so were you.

CHAPTER 1

AN EARLY START WITH A LOVING GOD

I believe the best place for me to start writing this booklet is from the beginning. My name is Gary Junious Davis. I was born here in Fayetteville, North Carolina. I can recall at a young age that I had very loving parents. I also had three sisters and two brothers. My family was very close. We were taught by our parents to love, respect, and support one another. We were all one young and happy family, and I was grateful for that.

My father worked hard to put food on our table and clothes on our backs. My siblings and I always had what we needed while growing up—thanks be to God, my mother, and my father.

My mother was a very loving, stay-at-home mom, who made it her duty to have breakfast ready for us each morning, get us dressed for school, help us with homework after school, and have us ready for bed at a certain time. Momma was an excellent cook, and I eagerly looked forward to meal time—especially during Thanksgiving, Christmas, and New Year's. I believe some of you know what I mean when I say that my dear mother, secondary to God, was my best friend. Momma and I were always intimately close. I knew deep down in my heart that I had a good mother; and I learned at an early age that I could talk to mom about anything, anytime, which meant a lot to me.

One thing I can recall about my childhood that was not pleasant at all was daddy chastising with his thick belt, and momma doing the same with those limbs from the bushes that she called switches. I did not like it then, but now I appreciate my parents for not sparing the rod.

I was not raised in a Christian home. There was very little talk about God in the home. As I grew up, one important and significant thing I can remember about my mother is that she always prayed before going to bed. Even more important to me is the fact that I can recall, at the young age of eleven or twelve, how close I felt to God. As a matter of fact, when my family and I would be watching television, I would also be praying. When we were outside playing hopscotch or dodgeball, I would be praying to God. I sincerely prayed at school and almost everywhere I went. I would find myself praying for peace of mind, for joy in life, for protection for my family and friends, and for the goodwill of all. I talked to the good Lord about my life and how I felt close to Him. The more I prayed and meditated on God, the more I would experience peace within and happiness. I considered God to be my best friend, and I truly enjoyed opening my heart to my best friend in prayer and in thankfulness.

In Matthew 19:13, God lets us know that parents brought their little children to Jesus "that he should put his hands on them and pray, and the disciples rebuked them." But Jesus said "suffer [allow] the little children and forbid them not to come unto me, for of such is the kingdom of heaven." Jesus is just as loving and compassionate a father to children of this day and age as He was in the Bible days. I came to the Lord as a youth in prayer and faith and He blessed me as I prayed to Him on a consistent basis; and God was in control every day of my life, of everything I said, including in my young life. I constantly prayed and meditated on God and was blessed daily by the grace of God. I was a grateful and content young boy. I know that back then God helped me with my prayers, and He answered my prayers. Oh, what a wonderful, loving, and awesome God He was and is! Hallelujah!

Let us, special readers, consider strongly what the Bible says, in 1 Thessalonians 5:16–18: "Rejoice evermore. Pray without ceasing. In every thing give thanks: for this is the will of God in Christ Jesus concerning you." This is exactly what God allowed me to do at that very young age. I believe God wants us all, no matter our age, to pray without ceasing so He can bless us even more without ceasing. That is just the kind of God He was to me and the kind of God He is. We should also consider that we do not always have to pray audibly because God knows all, including our hearts and our conscious thoughts and our unspoken meditative petitions. I also believe the more I talked and listened to God, the more faith in God I experienced. I felt very good and content because I knew that God was with me and for me. I also knew that God Almighty was only a prayer away. I believe that God loves it when we pray and that He is eager and pleased to answer our prayers.

I would like to make it clear at this point of my writing that God has a very special ear for the prayers of a true Christian, but He is not restricted to only answering the prayers of a true Christian. I believe that God is a God of grace and mercy for all, but especially His true followers who have accepted Him as their true Savior from sin.

In Luke 18:1, God informs us: "Then he [Jesus] spoke a parable to them to this end, that men ought always to pray, and not to faint." It says "men" in this scripture, but I believe everybody—including children—should always pray and not lose heart, even as I did as a child, by the grace of God. God loves all his children, regardless of our age. I am a witness that it can be a very dangerous thing to stop communing with God through prayer, meditation, and believing. I will write more about this in upcoming chapters, so keep reading.

It is vitally important for all of us to keep our requests before Jesus and keep our minds stayed on Him as I, by the grace of God, experienced at a young age but did not always continue to do. I would like to say in writing that, if we are not praying and if we do not maintain some type of a sincere relationship with God or Jesus Christ, then chances are we are fainting or losing heart with the God of hope, peace, and goodness.

Even more importantly, we should all give our lives to God—the One who created us in His image and the only one who gives us hope as well as life now and eternally. We all need a loving God to help us live right and be happily satisfied.

I write to all parents reading this: pray with and for your children. Teach them to pray because prayer changes things for the better and is, as it is said, the life of the soul.

Let me share with you a statement from the book *Steps to Christ,* written by Ellen White:

> Our heavenly Father waits to bestow upon us the fullness of His blessing. It is our privilege to drink largely at the fountain of boundless love. What a wonder it is that we pray so little! God is ready and willing to hear the sincere prayer of the humblest of His children, and yet there is much manifest reluctance on our part to make known our wants to God.

God shares with us, in Psalm 66:19, "But verily God hath heard me; he hath attended to the voice of my prayer." I am sincerely convinced that this scripture, containing the promise of God's hearing and attending to our prayers, was and is true in my life, and it can be true in your life as well. There is no reason to pray if we do not believe God hears our prayers.

I believe God has always had His hand on me, leading me to pray and have fellowship with Him. Even at this early stage in my life, I believed that God was real and true, that is, the God whom I knew and loved.

I also believed that God wanted me to give my heart and life to Him during those early years; but I did not do so. I know now that it is vitally important and essential for each of us to accept Him as our loving personal Savior from sin and get to know Him on a continual basis and to also get to know and trust God as soon as possible so that we can be blessed to the utmost as we experience His joy.

It is also very important for each of us to understand and know that God loves us all with an everlasting love and with lovingkindness He has drawn us (Jer. 31:3). God reaches toward us all with kindness motivated by a deep, eternal love, drawing us toward Himself. There is nobody who can love us like Jesus. Oh, if only we would all trust Him and take Him at His word! Jesus' dying for us as our substitute on that old rugged cross is love to the upmost; and it is an unlimited love that is not confined to bounds. The love of God, Jesus, and the Holy Spirit is also an unconditional love that is free for all who believe. Jesus Christ accepted our punishment, paid the price for our sins, and then offered us the new life that He had bought for us. That is definitely love supreme. I believe that, by His grace, I experienced some of that wonderful love He had for me early in my life, which I cherished, and I do not want to forget again because I once foolishly did.

If I should regret anything about my salvation it would be that I did not accept Jesus as my personal Savior at that young age. Let us remember, "now is the day of salvation" (2 Cor. 6:2).

The Bible informs us, in 2 Kings 22:1, 2: "Josiah was eight years old when he began to reign, and he reigned in Jerusalem one and thirty years. And he did that which was right in the sight of the LORD, and walked in all the ways of David his father, and declined neither to the right hand, nor to the left." Now, let me ask you a question: Do you think that King Josiah could have done that which was right in the sight of the Lord and conducted himself and lived in all the ways of his spiritual father David without a true communion with God and without a prayer-based relationship with God? I believe the answer is no, he could not. Josiah was a very young king who loved God, talked with God, and obeyed God. We may not be kings or queens, but we all should do as Josiah did. He, graciously and lovingly, obeyed God to the utmost, and so should we—and the sooner we do so, the better, I would say. Josiah was courageous and had a faithful relationship with God, and God blessed him because he had the young mind of Christ. Let us all be as determined to do God's will by trusting in Jesus, as the obedient young king did.

The Bible speaks of all flesh coming to God because He hears prayer without partiality (Ps. 65:2). This is why I could commune with Him at the age of twelve or thirteen. God is willing to listen to anybody and everybody's prayers about anything we want to tell Him. God is patient, kind, understanding, practical, merciful, and perfectly empathetic to all. Jesus Christ is a God who also forgives, intervenes, and provides for us. We should all praise and give Him thanks and all the glory because He strongly desires to share His goodness and love with those who get to know Him.

He has shown me that He has always loved me, even though I turned my back on Him and learned the hard way that I was born to die, in order to live.

I admonish you, special readers, to keep reading to find out more about this experience and to be blessed, hopefully, as you read.

CHAPTER 2

THE ACCIDENT DESIGNED BY THE DEVIL BUT BLESSED BY GOD

I was a grateful and content young boy. As I look back over my life, I can recall that I have really loved football and enjoyed playing. My daddy, my brothers, and I would watch football games on TV. Every Sunday afternoon we had a lot of fun and exciting times. At the age of 14, I played football for the Boys' Club Chargers. I played the quarterback position and was good at it. I loved running with the football and made a lot of touchdowns, or scores, for those reading that may not know a lot about football. I believe I played even better when my mom and dad came to see me play. I prayed about our games constantly. I believe God heard my prayers. We were champions of the league two years in a row. I can remember thanking God for blessing our football team.

I can also remember that one Saturday morning my friend Dwight and I were walking to the recreation center to play a game when we saw a person we knew driving a huge truck. The person driving the truck asked us if we wanted a ride. At that time, I considered something very important that my mother always told me and my siblings. Mama always told us not to ride with anyone she did not give us permission to ride with. I ignored that serious warning our mother gave us. So, my friend Dwight and I climbed into the large truck.

I would like to say in writing that it usually does us well to obey our mothers because, as a rule, they will not tell us to do anything wrong nor harmful. I would have you know, my friends, that my whole life was altered in a very negative and depriving way—all because I did not obey the wise advice of a loving mother. When Dwight and I got into the truck, we found out that the driver was drunk. We knew that it was not unusual for this person to be drunk, but not that early in the morning. I was very afraid as the reckless driver seemed to have fun scaring us with fast and dangerous driving. As the truck went around a curve, it began to turn over. Just then I thought about my football helmet but did not put it on because I did not want it to be known that I was scared about what might happen—and what did happen. I wanted to appear brave when I was very much afraid. Foolish and youthful pride is what I experienced, and it almost was the cause of my early death. I learned that, yes, pride does exist among the youth, and the devil is behind it all. I was a happy child who had a connection with Christ, but I was also arrogant and unwise when it came to protecting my head, in case of an accident, by simply putting on my helmet.

I would like to say in writing that God is the solution to our conceited ways, no matter what our age may be. We must realize that we are all born in sin, which can include being prideful— having an exaggerated high opinion of ourselves, which can only be conquered by Jesus Christ.

As a result of the truck turning over, I received a terrible head injury, which my helmet might have prevented had I not been so high-minded. I also experienced a terrible break to my leg. With the concussion of my brain as a result of the head injury, I went unconscious. The doctors told my mother that they did not know whether I would live or die. Praise be to God—a compassionate on-time God—I lived! Special readers, by the unmerited love of a wonderful God, I still live, move, and have my being, and I shout hallelujah, for I am grateful! I have been blessed by the best, and I praise God from whom all blessings flow!

I can imagine the devil was saying while I was in the coma, "I will kill him now and take him to hell with me when I go." But I can also imagine God saying, "Leave him alone! He is my child! He shall live because I love him. I have work for Gary to do, including the work of writing a booklet to the honor and glory of God." Amen. God is an awesome God, who is worthy to be praised, and I am surely convinced that God has the last say each day, even when it comes to life and death. Let us remember what Jesus said in Revelation 1:18, "I am he that liveth and was dead; and behold I am alive for evermore, Amen; and have the keys of hell and death." Praise God!

The doctor also told my mother, while I was still unconscious, that I could be paralyzed on one side, be deaf or dumb, or I could go blind as a result of the head injury. The devil was not finished with me yet, but we must remember that he is a liar. By the evil plan of the devil, I did go blind. I can recall having hope during this trying time. During the three days that I was blind, I remember praying, "Lord, I know that You know I am blind; so, if it be Your will, O Lord, please give me my eyesight back, but not my will, but Yours be done. In Jesus' name, amen." I believe that Jesus had guided me to have a prayer-based relationship with him during the previous days of my youth so I would be prepared to pray about my blindness and other things. As you probably have already figured out, yes, Jesus gave me my eyesight back. I now can see, praise God! I can see this pen I am writing with. I can see the paper I am writing on, and I am appreciative and grateful to Him! Hallelujah!

Now, during the time that I was blind, I was concerned about my blindness, but I was not worried. I can recall having hope and blind faith (smile). I believed in my heart that God could and would heal my eyes, if it were His will. Now I am a witness of what Jesus says in Matthew 7:7, "Ask, and it shall be given you; seek, and ye shall find; knock, and it shall be opened unto you." This promise is true. The one thing I can say regarding this and all other scriptures is that Jesus Christ is a promise-keeper. I am a witness because I can see again. Hallelujah! I am happy that I had hope and believed in my heart that Jesus could heal my eyes. In the book of Hebrews, chapter 11, verse 6, God informs us, "Without faith it is impossible to please him." It is very simple, special readers. If you desire to please God, you must believe Him. God will surely bless you and will help you to see that He is better than good; He will cause you to see that He is great. There is nobody that can bless us and make us satisfied and happy like Jesus, and you know what? Jesus will never let us down nor forsake us. Jesus Christ of Nazareth is the great physician, and He is still in the healing business today, just as He was in biblical days. He is still the Lord our God who changes not.

God shares with us, in Luke 18:41–43, what Jesus said to the blind man, "What wilt thou that I shall do unto thee? And he said, Lord, that I may receive my sight. And Jesus said unto him, Receive thy sight: thy faith hath saved thee. And immediately he received his sight, and followed him, glorifying God: and all the people, when they saw it, gave praise unto God." Thanks be to God that the same healing spiritual power that was manifested by Jesus in the Scriptures is the same healing power He used to heal my eyes some 48 years ago. I wish that I could say I have been following Jesus ever since that time, but I have not. I thank God for the true biblical fact that His Son Jesus has been very patient with me, not willing that I should perish, and the same goes for you. Jesus desires for all of us to be followers of Him because, when we are, we can follow him right into His heavenly kingdom. And that makes following Him worthwhile and one of the best things we can ever do!

The devil also tried to take my right leg from me. The doctor told my mother that, if a skin graft for my leg where the bone popped out of my skin did not work, then they would have to amputate my leg. The doctor had determined that if the skin graft did not work then my leg would become infected. I had the skin graft and was sent home for about ten days. When I returned to the hospital, the doctor told my mama and I that the skin graft was a success. Hallelujah! I considered this good news and an answer to much prayer because I was very sincerely praying from my heart daily. To this day I still have the lower part of my right leg, by the healing power of Jesus Christ, our prayer-answering God, and, yes, He is worthy to be praised. Hallelujah!

In John 14:13, 14, Jesus Christ himself shares with us, "And whatsoever ye shall ask in my name, that will I do, that the Father may be glorified in the Son. If ye ask any thing in my name, I will do it." Jesus has unlimited resources to answer prayers of faith, according to His divine will. Oh, what an on-time, faithful, and loving compassionate God He is! Let us remember that the Lord is good, His mercy is everlasting, and His truth endures to all generations (Ps. 100:5).

God has made me a believer, by proving Himself to me, healing me, and sparing my life above all. What a wonder-working God He has been to me! What about you? Jesus Christ loves us, this I know, for the Bible, along with His miraculous healing blessings towards me, tells me so. What about you, special readers? What about you?

At this point of my writing to you, I would like to share with you a vision God gave me. God gave me this vision after I regained consciousness and after He gave me back my eyesight. I can recall that I had an older roommate. He was a Caucasian man who had reddish skin. As I looked at the man, who had his shirt off, he became red as he smoked his cigarette. Eventually his face and body turned into an image of the devil. The devil that I observed looked like some of the pictures I had seen of the devil. I realized, after studying my Bible much more, that the devil is not red from head to toe and does not really have a pitchfork, standing in the middle of consuming fire. I think the good Lord allowed me to see the image of the devil the way He did so that I could be sure to recognize him as the devil I knew at my young age. The image of the devil was waving his hand in a motion for me to join him in the lake of fire. He was also laughing at me as he terrified me. I was so frightened that I jumped out of the hospital bed with all the tubes attached to me. I also had a cast from my thigh down to my foot on my right leg.

The nurses rushed into my room to see what was going on. I just stood there afraid and wobbling as they put me back into the bed. I noticed that the nurses could not see what I saw in vision. The laughing and torturing devil was still there enjoying me being full of fear and panic. One reason I was so scared was because I did not know what would happen if this was to continue. I was very alarmed and annoyed. I was full of terror. For some reason, I decided to turn my head the other way. To my surprise, I saw the image of a man. I soon recognized that the image was Jesus Christ. I was still afraid at first glance, but then said to myself, *This is the Savior! This is Jesus Christ, and I have no reason to be afraid.* I knew who Jesus was because He looked like He did on some of the pictures I had seen of Him. He had brownish wooly hair; His eyes had flames of fire in them. He had a halo around His head as well. His face was pale, and He had on a white robe that was as white as snow. Jesus also had little angels revolving around his head. I became very relaxed and comfortable as I gazed at such a beautiful and glorious sight. I felt as if I were in a trance as I continued to look with amazing delight. After about two minutes, I suppose, the marvelous and gorgeous sight of Jesus began to disappear. After the image of Jesus was gone, I wondered if the image of the devil was still there. I turned my head back the other way, and, lo and behold, the devil was gone too. I saw my roommate again. What a relief and blessing that was for me. What a mighty God we serve—or should serve! God is better than good; He is majestic and marvelous in my eyes. What about yours? How do you see Jesus?

I can recall asking the Lord if there was any interpretation or message related to the vision I had. I believe the Lord spoke to me and said, "Gary, as long as you keep your eyes on me, you do not have to be afraid of the devil because eventually the devil will flee." The devil is a defeated foe because of what Jesus has done for us on Calvary's cross. The devil has *some* power, but Jesus Christ has *all* power. May you find him now if you have not. The devil desires to take us all to hell's lake a fire with him when that time comes. We do not have to worry about the lake of fire if we look to Jesus daily and continue in faith after we have accepted Him as our personal Savior.

Jesus is real, and so is the devil. We must remember that there is a great controversy going on right now between good and evil, and humanity is in the middle. The devil hates us and desires to scare and torture us, as he did me when I was in the hospital. The victory over sin and Satan is ours, for the devil is no match for Jesus. Oh, what a mighty God He is!

I thank Jesus for being there for me when I needed Him most, especially when I was in the coma. I loved Jesus then, and I love Him now because He saved my life, gave me my eyesight back, and healed my leg, and because He gave me a literal vision of Himself and His power over Satan.

There is another miracle I would like to share with you at this time. I have had a history of mental illness since I was approximately 18 years old. I was diagnosed with schizophrenia along with manic depression. At the age of approximately thirty, when I was a member of Parks Chapel Freewill Baptist Church, I became very mentally sick and very, very depressed. I became suicidal and attempted to take my own life because I felt that God had abandoned me, and I had lost all my hope in Jesus. To make a long story short, I took a lot of pills from the medicine cabinet. I can recall getting on my knees and praying that Jesus would forgive me for taking my own life. I asked Jesus to somehow and in some way allow me to go to heaven. I became dizzy, and I sat up on the couch where I slept at my mother's house. My sister Angie got up out of bed for some reason and saw me sitting up and told my mother that she should get up and check on me, and mama did. Mama asked me what I was doing sitting up so early in the morning, and I believe it was about one or two o'clock in the morning. I was always honest with mama, and I told her that I had taken many different kinds of pills from the medicine cabinet. Mama rushed over to the apartment of our neighbor and good friend Roma and told her what had happened and that I needed to go to the emergency room. All I could remember was laying down in the back seat of Roma's car. When I regained consciousness, they had pumped my stomach to remove the pills. Mama told me that the doctor said that, if I had gotten to the emergency room a half hour later, I would have died. All I can say to you, special readers, is praise God and hallelujah for His intervening mercy and grace, which was right on time! I am very pleased and grateful to share with you that, by the grace of God, I am not suicidal anymore, and I have not been suicidal for a long, long time. Thank you, Jesus, my best and loving friend! I give Him glory and praise that only He deserves. What a loving and merciful God He is! Hallelujah! Will you praise Him with me? Hallelujah! Jesus Christ is able and worthy. He loves us all. The Bible says, in Psalm 150:6, "Let every thing that hath breath praise the Lord." Let us give him the highest praise because there is none like Him. We were created to praise the Lord, and giving Him praise, honor, glory, thanks, and exaltation should be our continuous delight.

CHAPTER 3

RUNNING FROM JESUS

I can recall that, after I got out of the hospital, the gracious and good God spoke to me saying, "Gary, go to the church and tell my people there what great things I have done for you." I knew the Lord was directing me to go to Parks Chapel Free Will Baptist Church. As I mentioned earlier, I had gone there before as a child. My response to the Lord was somewhat like Jeremiah's response to his calling. I said to the Lord, "Lord, I cannot do what You desire for me to do because I am young and afraid. The people at Parks Chapel Church will not listen to me because I am only a child." The Lord continued to command me to go to the church and to share my testimony, but I would only try to ignore the Lord's calling. I knew it was the Lord Jesus speaking to me because I had heard that still, peaceful, and small voice speak to me many times before, but I would not obey.

Eventually, I graduated from E. E. Smith High School, here in Fayetteville, North Carolina. My life began to take a drastic turn for the worse. After I graduated, I did not have any goals, achievements, or career in mind to pursue. I felt that all I needed to do was to graduate and eventually everything else would fall into place. I would like to say to any young people reading who may be about to graduate from high school: Set some valuable goals for yourself. Decide what you would like to achieve in life. Plan for a career that you would like to pursue. Most importantly, pray to the good Lord about these decisions. Then strive to obtain your big dreams, according to His divine purpose. I settled for a minimum paying job that I did not care for. It was better than nothing, but only a little better. God would have us to dream big and to do great things.

With nothing to pursue or strive for after graduating, I experienced a lot of hardship, troubles, and even some dangerous times. I began to drink and became an alcoholic. I started drinking because everybody else I hung around was drinking. My alcoholic drinking led to me becoming a thief, liar, robber, and a very violent, law-breaking jailbird. I became pitiful and a disgrace to myself and to society. I was hopeless. I did not plan to be this way, but this is what happens when we are idle and unproductive in life, and, above all, when we turn away from the Lord our God. I did not plan this for my life, but the devil had a plan for me. I chose to follow that plan, totally unaware where it would lead me.

In the book of Romans 6:16, God lets us know, "Know ye not, that to whom ye yield yourselves servants to obey, his servants ye are to whom ye obey; whether of sin unto death, or of obedience unto righteousness?" God also informs us, special readers, in Deuteronomy 28:15–24, that the disobedient will be cursed. I can truly say that I was a true witness of this; the devil tried to kill me. I eventually did not hear the voice of the Lord telling me to go to church to share my testimony because my drinking and all the foolishness that came along with it drew me further and further away from God, which was and is not a good thing to do.

I can recall going to a neighborhood convenience store where I would go back to the alcoholic beverages section. Once there, I would grab a couple of six-packs of beer and dash out of the store. I would then jump into the waiting car that my cousin was driving, and we would be off to the races. How stupid and what a lawless, crazy thing to do! I can see this clearly now, but back then this kind of sinful behavior was part of my wicked lifestyle of running from Jesus. I believe in my heart I was looking for the peace of mind and happiness that I once had when I was not running from Jesus' calling me to be a witness for him. I thought I knew what was best for me, but I was deceived.

Alcoholism became my god and master. My heavy drinking led to my not being able to keep a job. Eventually, I became a bum and a street person. I did a lot of crazy and evil things that bought harm to myself and others. All I wanted to do was to try to drink my problems away, but, special readers, it did not work. I was in bad shape because of my every-day-and-night drinking. I hated people because I hated myself. Drinking only made things worse. Though I only drank for five years, the devil almost killed me during that period of shameful drunkenness.

I recall going to the doctor with my mother for a regular check-up. The doctor told me that, if I did not stop drinking, I would die from cirrhosis of the liver. He told me that about two-thirds of my liver had already deteriorated because of my raging alcoholic drinking. Very foolishly, I had continued to drink because I could not help myself, and the devil, through drinking, had a strong hold on me. He was determined to kill me; *he* was in control.

God let us know, in Proverbs 20:1, "Wine is a mocker, strong [intoxicating] drink is raging; and whosoever is deceived thereby is not wise." When God says "mocker," according to this scripture, He means that intoxicating drinking becomes a deceiver, impostor, and scorner, and that sounds like the devil himself to me. Who does that sound like to you?

In the book of Isaiah, chapter 28, verse 7, God says intoxicating drinking causes a person to stumble in judgment. This tells me why I made so many bad and harmful decisions. It was because my judgment was not of God but of the devil, working through my strong drinking. I was in darkness. Eventually, as a result of my drinking, I was arrested twice. I was charged with two counts of breaking and entering as well as larceny. When my court date came up, I was scared. I did not want to go to prison because I had heard about some of the things that happened to people while in prison. (My friend, who was guilty of the same crime as I, had already been sent to prison.) I knew I was not the prison type, even though I was a guilty criminal. As I fearfully waited for my court date to come, I did something that I had stopped doing—I prayed a lot with a serious, contrite spirit, which included humbly asking God to forgive me for all I had done that did not please Him. I knew truly what alcoholism had done to my life. I also realized that the only way I could be delivered from going to prison would be by a miracle performed by Jesus Christ, whom had I been running from. Instead of running from God and Jesus, I should have been running to Parks Chapel Church, as Jesus had commanded me to do many years before. Running from my Lord and Savior Jesus Christ led to a lot of painful, troublesome hardships. I found myself in a position from which I could only turn to Jesus for help. I also knew deep down in my heart that it would take a power outside of myself—and not any human power—to deliver me from going to prison. My only hope was Jesus. If only He would help me one more time.

CHAPTER 4

AN ON-TIME GOD

After I had spent a lot of time in serious contemplation and prayer, my court date finally arrived. I was asked by my public defender if I wanted him to defend me or if I wanted to speak for myself. I chose to speak for myself, and I took my seat on the witness stand and was sworn in. I was very frightened. After a short period of dialogue by the court officials and the judge, I was asked by the judge what I had to say for myself. My response was as follows: "I am guilty of the crimes I am charged with. I should be sent to prison. I have stopped drinking. I am also going to an alcoholic rehabilitation clinic. I never got in trouble by breaking the law until I was under the influence of alcohol. I, therefore, ask that I not be sent to prison. I ask the judge and jury to give me another chance in life. Please do not send me to prison." Hesitating, the judge finally responded, "This young man has told us that he is guilty and that he has done wrong. He has also told us that he is trying to help himself by seeking alcoholic rehabilitation treatment. He is asking for a chance to start over in life, to do things differently. All charges are dropped, with three years of probation." Praise God! Hallelujah! I began to weep as I rejoiced because I knew that God had answered my prayers once again. What a Majestic and wonder-working God He is, who is always right on time! I believed from my heart that God had worked a miracle for me. I was amazed and grateful. As I was waiting to be released, a district attorney approached me and said, "I just do not understand what has happened here. You were supposed to be on your way to prison. This is very unusual." I looked him straight in the eye and said, "I know exactly what has happened here today. I have been set free because I have been praying that God would deliver me from going to prison, and He has heard me. That is why I am weeping tears of joy and gratitude. I could not deliver myself, but God, through His Son, who I prayed to, could and did."

That was nothing but unselfish, unlimited, unconditional, and empathetic love. Have you ever experienced it? I tell you there is nothing like it because He is infinitely merciful. And I will shout it from the rooftops. There is none like Him!

God had blessed me again like only He could. My heart was full of joy and appreciation for my good Lord and for what He had done for me. It was also good to know that He was still blessing me despite my past sinful and rebellious ways. He is worthy to be exalted. I am convinced that the Son of God, Jesus, to whom I prayed that day in the courtroom, is a powerful, omnipresent and all-knowing Lord who is still in the prayer-answering business—even after I had rejected Him and grieved the Holy Spirit!

In 2 Chronicles 7:14, God shares with us, "If my people, which are called by my name, shall humble themselves, and pray, and seek my face, and turn from their wicked ways; then will I hear their prayer from heaven, and will forgive their sin, and heal their land." I began to cease running away from God, but I still needed grace and mercy in order to become a true follower of Christ. I still needed to become a baptized member in His remnant church. I still needed to be converted, sanctified, and filled with the Holy Spirit. I most surely needed to die to anything that was hindering me from receiving these blessings from a loving and kind God. I still needed a new heart and spirit that the Lord has promised to Christians in Ezekiel 36:26. I needed to become more Christ-like and become saved. The only way I could obtain all these blessings would be by God's unmerited favor through His only begotten Son Jesus, who is better—so much better—than good. He is great! Essentially, I needed more of Jesus and less of myself. In order to be happy and content, I needed to stop living according to the devil's deceitful evil ways. In that still worldly nature I was born into, I realized that Jesus was an on-time God, a promise-keeping and good Lord. Jesus had proven Himself to me. This had a lot to do with His causing me to continue to die so that I could live.

CHAPTER 5

CONTINUING TO DIE TO SELF AND THE FLESH

Immediately after God had delivered me from going to prison, my alcohol abuse counselor sent me to a good alcoholic rehabilitation center in Greenville, North Carolina. My counselor told me that he was not sending me there because I needed treatments but because I would enjoy it. My counselor was exactly right. I did enjoy it—every bit of my six weeks there. I did not feel alone in my recovery anymore because there were others with the same disease I had. The counselors and all the other people I met at the center were very nice and respectful. I learned a lot about alcoholism and myself. I left the center with an even stronger desire to never drink again.

After returning home from treatment, I eventually stopped hanging around with my old friends that were still drinking. I recall asking God to please keep me sober one day at a time, as I was counseled to do while in treatment. I enjoyed being sober and talking to family members and friends in the neighborhood. I especially enjoyed conversing with my mother who was my best friend. Mama brought out the best in me. She was on my side and by my side with loving support.

As a result of daily prayer, I begin to feel a closeness to Jesus. I also considered what Jesus had done for me daily. Contemplating what Jesus had done for me and His goodness towards me gave me strength and courage to live without drinking—one day at a time. I knew deep down within my heart that, if I went back to drinking, I would most surely die. A friend I met at the alcohol and rehabilitation center invited me to an A. A. (Alcoholics Anonymous) meeting. I went to the meeting here in Fayetteville, North Carolina, and was tremendously blessed. I slowly took the twelve steps of A.A., which were spiritually designed to help a recovering alcoholic maintain his or her sobriety. I enjoyed the different meetings of A.A. and especially enjoyed and was blessed by the open discussion Friday night meeting. All the meetings were designed to help the alcoholic in recovery.

After being a member of Alcoholics Anonymous for two years, I eventually got a job at a local alcoholic and drug addict treatment center called "The Life Center of Fayetteville." My job title was "Alcoholic and Drug Abuse Counselor, in-training." Eventually on my job, I met a nice Christian lady named Christine. Christine really admired me for my prayer life and for my spiritual knowledge and understanding. One day Christine took me to meet her pastor. She told him about me and my spiritual characteristics. The pastor told us that there was a battle between Christ and Satan going on for my life. He told us that he believed Christ would win the battle and that I would be a Christian one day. I have always remembered the conversation and the prayer he extended to me. I left the pastor's home a blessed young man with a lot to consider from a spiritual perspective.

I was doing well without the alcohol in my system, but I still had a lot of spiritual growing to do. And I still had a lot of dying to do, and only Jesus could help me. I still needed to die to other sins besides being a drunkard and a thief. I still needed the power of Jesus to cause me to die to committing fornication, speaking profanity, being envious of others, hating people without a cause, being judgmental of others, being selfish, and having low self-esteem.

After I started reading the Bible at Christine's request, I was enlightened and blessed by the grace of God. I began to understand what living God's way was all about. I wanted to live and please the good Lord. I begin to pray about my fleshly, sinful, and worldly nature that I had been born into. The devil wanted me to continue committing these sins, but Jesus began to work as my Deliverer, and, by His sufficient grace, I stopped fornicating, speaking profanity, and being envious of others. Eventually, by the mercies of Jesus, I stopped hating people. I also died to being judgmental and having low self-esteem. Jesus gets all the glory for changing me from the inside out. I could not have done this for myself, for we do not have the power to change ourselves. If we ourselves could change and turn from our wicked ways, then Jesus would not have had to come and die for us as our substitute. Jesus Christ is the only one who qualifies to transform our characters to reflect His character. He is the one who died for us on that old rugged cross.

I began to grow more spiritually as I read the Bible, and I continued to die, losing the desires of my evil nature. As I continued to read my Bible and pray, I felt myself, by the grace of God, being drawn from the grip of the devil into the presence of the living God. In Romans 6:1, 2, God says, by way of Paul, "What shall we say then? Shall we continue in sin that grace may abound? God forbid. How shall we, that are dead to sin [in my case, dying to sin], live any longer therein?" I began to desire freedom from sin's power. I desired to live an upright lifestyle. I wanted to do right according to God's will. I knew that, if I would go back to drinking and sin, I would surely die in my sin. Thanks be to God that I was headed in a new direction! I begin to feel very close to God again, and I was loving it.

In Romans 8:8, God informs us that "they that are in the flesh [the sinful worldly nature] cannot please God." In other words, we all should, by the grace of God, die to sin in order to live righteously according to God's divine will and way. My character was becoming more and more like that of Christ. My personage began to reflect Jesus in character.

CHAPTER 6

REALLY LIVING BY THE GRACE OF GOD

I always considered what Christine constantly encouraged me to do. She would always humbly invite me to give my life to the good Lord and become a Christian. She would also often tell me that I was very close to becoming a Christian. Along with Christine's pleadings, my sister Janice and my friend Angela would also try very diligently to lead me to the good Lord. One day, Janice dared me to become a Christian. I had been attending Parks Chapel Church on a regular basis with Janice. One Sunday, I, by the grace of God, responded to an appeal by the assistant pastor. I became a Christian that day, and I also responded to Janice's dare, which I had not forgotten. I was twenty-eight years old when I finally accepted Jesus Christ as my personal Savior. Praise God and to Him belongs all the glory! I was asked by the assistant pastor to kneel at the altar and pray to the good Lord about what I had just done. He said that he had never asked anybody to do that before. He also asked me to lift my hands towards heaven and give Jesus praise. I experienced a very inspirational and reviving spirit that came over me as I praised Jesus with all my heart for what He had done for me. I knew I had finally done what the Lord wanted me to do years ago as a child. I had, by the grace of God, come home where I belonged. I was thankful to the Lord and full of joy. It is the best thing I ever did.

I remind you, special readers, that Parks Chapel Church was the church where God had earlier commanded me to go to let His people know by testimony what He had done for me while in the hospital after the truck accident. It was years later, but shortly after becoming a member of the church, I began to testify. I told the people at church how God, after the head injury, healed my leg and eyes after being blind for three days. I even testified about the vision I had of the Lord and the devil. I shared with them the interpretation of the vision also. I testified of the goodness of the Lord frequently and was blessed each time I did. I had finally done what Jesus desired for me, and I found joy and peace within because I was obedient to the good Lord, who had done so much for me.

As I continued to attend church on Sunday and Tuesday nights, I found myself growing swiftly in my Christian journey. My prayer life and my study of the Bible became very important to me, as I enjoyed hungering and thirsting after righteousness. I enthusiastically began to enjoy true communion and true conversion with my good Lord, reminding me of my childhood with the good Lord but more of a blessing. One of the first of many scriptures that I really liked was Hebrews 11:1: "Now faith is the substance of things hoped before, the evidence of things not seen." I believed by faith that I would receive the assurance of things I hoped for but did not actually see until I got an answer to my prayer, by the grace of God. God gave me evidence, such as the healing of my eyesight, my experiencing sobriety, and much more.

I began to become acquainted with the promises of God in the Bible, such as John 3:16. "For God so loved the world, that he gave his only begotten Son, that whosoever believeth in him should not perish, but have everlasting life." My faith began to grow even more as I studied and realized that surely the Lord was able, that He was who He said He was, and that He would do what He said He would do according to His holy Word.

Sin began to lose its grip on me and my life. It was also very much a blessing to know that, if I would confess my sins, Jesus would forgive my sins and cleanse me from all unrighteousness. Oh, how thankful and appreciative I became of the holy Word of God! By the grace of God, I began to pattern my life according to the Bible. I began to really live as

Christ would have me to live—according to His will and way. I had several reasons to praise God from whom all blessings flow. I walked and talked with the good Lord just as I did as a young child but with a closer relationship with Him as He opened my eyes to behold the Scriptures.

After being a member of Parks Chapel Free Will Baptist church a few years, I still felt that I was missing something on my Christian journey with Jesus. Just before becoming a deacon, something very important, something significant and very impressive took place in my life. One nice summer day I found myself sitting at my mother's kitchen table reading my Bible, as I often did. I happened to turn in my Bible to Isaiah 58:13, 14, which caught my attention for some reason. Isaiah 58:13, 14 reads, and God informs us: "If thou turn away thy foot from the sabbath, from doing thy pleasure on my holy day, and call the sabbath a delight; the holy of the LORD, honorable; and shalt honour him, not doing thine on ways, nor finding thine own pleasure, nor speaking thine own words; then shalt thou delight thyself in the LORD; and I will cause thee to ride upon the high places of the earth, and feed thee with the heritage of Jacob thy father; for the mouth of the LORD hath spoken it." I recall that, after reading these scriptures, I had a strong conviction to pray. My prayer, which I still remember to this day as if it was yesterday, went something like this: "Lord, if there is a church today that worships on this Sabbath day, help me to find that church so I can become a member and experience the promises of verse 14. In Jesus' name I pray, Amen." To make a long story short, a few days after that prayer I met a nice young lady named Sheila at Fayetteville State University where both of us attended. Right from the beginning of our conversation we talked about the goodness of the Lord. Sheila gave me a tract, a small piece of Christian literature, entitled "The Sabbath, a Sign of God's Rulership." I read the tract and was truly blessed. The tract told me a lot about the sabbath day, including what was the biblical day to keep holy. I learned, by the grace of God, that the Sabbath day, the day of rest and worship, is on the seventh day of the week, Saturday, and not on the first day of the week, Sunday. (Please see Genesis 2:1–3 and Exodus 20:8–11.) The tract was small but very powerful and inspiring.

Sheila invited me to the Seventh-day Adventist Church where we attended Sabbath school (like Sunday school) and divine worship. I enjoyed the services with gratitude and thanksgiving to God. Sheila also invited me to a Revelation Seminar. I went with her and was glad I did because I learned so much. All that I learned was straight from the Bible. I also realized that I was hungering and thirsting for more truth according to the Bible in which, by the grace of God, I found at Abney Chapel Seventh-day Adventist Church here in Fayetteville, North Carolina.

Some of the new truths that I learned were the true state of the dead (see 1 Thess. 4:16, 17), the truth about the Sabbath (see Exod. 20:8–11; Isa. 58:13, 14; Acts 16:13; Gen. 2:1–3); God's free health plan (see 3 John 2; John 11:10; Gen. 1:29); and the return of Christ (see Heb. 9:28; John 14:3; Rev. 1:7). God also taught me more about the Ten Commandments and not just nine of the ten (see 1 John 3:4; Prov. 3:1, 2). I learned many more inspiring teachings, all according to the Holy Bible, and I was grateful. Praise God, I was being taught the truth, and the truth was freeing me from error! During the time we were attending the seminar, I went to the bishop one Sunday after church. I had been convicted by the Holy Spirit about the true biblical seventh-day Sabbath, the holy day of rest and worship. There was no doubt in my mind that the good Lord was leading me to join the Seventh-day Adventist Church. After entering the bishop's office, I told him that God, by His Spirit, was leading me to become a Seventh-day Adventist. He listened to me and then asked me a very important question: Was I sure that God and the Holy Spirit were leading me to become a Seventh-day Adventist? I responded with a very firm, "Yes, I do." Then the bishop told me that there was nothing he could do to stop me. He wished me the best by the grace of God.

The basic biblical health plan I just mentioned includes (1) fresh air, (2) diet, (3) water—external and internal, (4) abstinence, (5) exercise, (6) temperance, (7) rest, and (8) trust in God. What comfort and joy these eight laws of health have brought me while improving my health, by the grace of God! I thank God also for Pastor Hatcher, who the Lord used in a mighty and inspiring way through the seminar. I also found out, by God's grace, that the Seventh-day Adventist Church is God's true remnant church (see Rev. 22:14, which describes keeping *all* of God's Ten Commandments; see also Rev. 12:7; 19:10; 14:6–12; John 14:15). The Seventh-day Adventist Church is God's last-day true remnant church because its doctrines are identical with the first Apostolic church, according to the Bible.

I do not write this with the intention of offending anyone in churches other than the Seventh-day Adventist Church. I do not fight against flesh and blood, but I will tell the truth as God has taught me. God has His true followers in every denomination, but He desires for all of them to come up a little higher by the grace of God (Rev. 18:1–4). After the Revelation Seminar, by the grace of God, I became a baptized member of the Seventh-day Adventist Church, and I am grateful for my new lifestyle according to the doctrines of the Seventh-day Adventist movement, which is not a cult. I am blessed and pleased about being a Seventh-day Adventist, and I know that I am in the church that God would have me to be. Remember, I read and prayed my way into the Seventh-day Adventist Church, according to Isaiah 58:13, 14. Man did not and I did not put myself in this church. Nobody therefore will run me out. I desired to become a Seventh-day Adventist before I knew anything about it because God is good. I don't feel as though I am missing something spiritually important anymore because I have been exposed to the whole truth of the Bible and nothing but the truth. I do not say in writing that the Seventh-day Adventist Church is a perfect church, but it is God's last day remnant church. That means that it follows all the biblical requirements of God's true doctrines (Rev. 12:14). Please bear in mind that a woman represents the church, both the defiled church (Rev. 17) and the pure church (Rev. 12), which are the false church and God's true church.

I was blessed in the Baptist Church, but I could not find the biblical truth there. Because the whole truth according to the Bible was not taught there. We must remember, my friends, that truth mixed with error is error, which is not of God. I love the people in my former Baptist church, and I love the people in all churches, though I do not agree with some of their doctrines or teachings contrary to biblical truth. Shortly after joining the Seventh-day Adventist Church, I became a deacon in training. Eventually I became an ordained deacon. By the grace of God, I became the Personal Ministries leader, which is the director of outreach work of the church. Later I found myself ministering in the Street Corner Ministry by the grace of God. I also did nursing home ministry, jail ministry, prayer band leader ministry, community service ministry, radio ministry, and "A Closer View" (a self-supporting ministry) over the years. I consider all I have done for the Lord in the Seventh-day Adventist Church really living. Glory and honor and praise to Jesus Christ who has worked in me through the Holy Spirit to do of His good pleasure! I love preaching and, by the grace of God, I have done a lot of preaching in different churches; and, special readers, I tell you the truth, I am genuinely living for Jesus Christ, and I love it. There is nothing like it!

Before I could do, by the grace of God, all this ministering for Jesus, there was something that had to take place in my life that was very important and necessary. I had to die daily to a lot of selfish and evil sins. I had to die to an unrighteous sinful lifestyle before I could live righteously by faith in Jesus Christ and serve Him. I know what Paul means when he says, in 1 Corinthians 15:31, "I die daily." We are, I say in writing once again, born in sin; therefore, we must die to sin in order to really live for Christ and serve Him as He fits us for eternal life. I could not minister to others when I hated others because Jesus says we should love others. So, I had to die with the help of the Lord. I had to die to hating others. It is the same with all other sins that I or anyone else has. We cannot die to sin on our own because we did not die for our sins on the cross—Jesus did. Jesus is the Author and Finisher of our salvation. He is the deliverance from sin because He is the only one that causes us to experience salvation and truly live now and forever. Jesus Christ is very willing and able to wash us thoroughly from our sins and cleanse us from all unrighteousness and make us happy in the process.

If you, special reader, have not given your life to Jesus Christ and accepted him as your personal Savior from sin, if you have not experienced the joy of salvation by way of an intimate relationship with God, what are you waiting for? Now is the day of salvation. Do not let eternal life pass you by. Jesus is waiting, ready to save you, as He has saved me and millions of other people like you. Let us always remember what God lets us know in 1 John 5:11–13 (NKJV), "And this is the testimony: that God has given us eternal life, and this life is in His Son. He who has the Son has life; he who does not have the Son of God does not have life. These things I have written to you who believe in the name of the Son of God, that you may know you have eternal life, and that you may continue to believe in the name of the Son of God."

I was once lost, but now, by the grace of God, I am found. I was once blinded by sin, but now I see. I am authentically living, and I am loving it— all because of Jesus, who has always been there for me. What about you?

CHAPTER 7

BORN TO DIE IN ORDER TO LIVE, ACCORDING TO THE BIBLE

I will now briefly share with you what it is to be born to die in order to live, according to the Bible. Psalm 51:5 (NKJV) reads, "Behold I was brought forth in iniquity [lawlessness], and in sin did my mother conceive me." God informs us, according to this scripture, that we are all, like David, born in sin. Our natural tendency is to sin, and without a redeeming Lord and Savior, we remain in our sinfulness, and our sin continues to dominate us, leading to death, even the second death in hell's lake of fire after judgment (Rev. 20:14, 15). Since we are all born in sin, we all need to be born again. In John 3:3, Jesus tells Nicodemus and us as well that we must be born again if we are going to make it into heaven. We must all be personally born again, by a grace-faith personal relationship with Jesus Christ based on the Word of God. He tells us that the treasures of wickedness profit nothing, but righteousness delivers from death (Prov. 10:2). We need to base our doing good and right and our really living on a power and source other than ourselves because God informs us, in Isaiah 64:6: "But we are all like an unclean thing, and all our righteousness are like filthy rags," and filthy rags cannot change or save us. Jesus is the Way, the Truth, and the Life. By having faith in Jesus and what He has done, is doing, and will do for us, we really and truly live by becoming sanctified and saved. We must live by faith in Jesus because He is our qualified source of hope, strength, redemption, and life more abundantly now and forever and ever. God lets us know, in 2 Corinthians 5:14, 15: "For the love of Christ constraineth us; because we thus judge, that if one died for all, then were all dead: and that he died for all, that they which live should not henceforth live unto themselves, but unto him which died for them, and rose again." We must all be like Paul and continue to die to sin daily in the new-birth experience by the grace of God and by faith in Jesus Christ. We must understand and know that sanctification is a gradual and continuous process until we die or until Jesus returns, whichever comes first and so be it.

In closing, I say unto you, remember that by depending on Jesus we can and must die to sin, self, and Satan. By believing in Jesus, we can experience true life and life eternal in the new heaven and earth. By trusting Jesus, we can be transformed through the renewing of our minds. We can really live right as the blood of Jesus cleanses us from sin and causes us to stop living in sin. As my sister dared me, I now dare you to give Jesus a try. I know that you won't regret giving your heart and life to Jesus because He desires to satisfy you and make you happy as He saves you from sin. I love you all, be blessed, and thank you for reading.

www.ingramcontent.com/pod-product-compliance
Lightning Source LLC
LaVergne TN
LVHW021549080426
835509LV00019B/2923